# AN OLD FASHIONED
# THANKSGIVING

## Louisa May Alcott

Applewood Books
Bedford, Massachusetts

*An Old-Fashioned Thanksgiving* was originally published in 1882.

ISBN 978-1-55709-135-2

Thank you for purchasing an Applewood Book. Applewood reprints America's lively classics—books from the past that are still of interest to modern readers. For a free copy of our current catalog, please write to Applewood Books, Box 365, Bedford, MA 01730.

**Library of Congress Cataloging-in-Publication Data**
Alcott, Louisa May, 1832-1888.              ·
    An old-fashioned Thanksgiving / Louisa May Alcott.
      p.     cm.
    Summary: Follows the activities of seven children in nineteenth-century New England as they prepare for the Thanksgiving holiday while Mother is away caring for Grandmother.
    ISBN 978-1-55709-135-2
    [1. Family life—Fiction.    2. Thanksgiving Day—Fiction.   3. New England—Fiction.]  I. Title.
[PZ7.A3350m     1993]
[Fic]–dc20                     93-36951
                                       CIP
                                       AC

# AN OLD FASHIONED THANKSGIVING

# An Old Fashioned Thanksgiving

Many years ago, up among the New Hampshire hills, lived Farmer Bassett, with a house full of sturdy sons and daughters growing up about him. They were poor in money, but rich in land and love, for the wide acres of wood, corn, and pasture land fed, warmed, and clothed the flock, while mutual patience, affection, and courage made the old farm-house a very happy home.

November had come; the crops were in, and barn, buttery, and bin were overflowing with the harvest that rewarded the summer's hard work The big kitchen was a jolly place just now, for in the great fire-place roared a cheerful fire; on the walls hung garlands of dried apples, onions, and corn; up aloft from the beams shone crook-necked squashes, juicy hams, and dried venison—for in those days deer still haunted the deep forests, and hunters flourished. Savory smells were in the air; on the crane hung steaming kettles, and down among the red embers copper sauce-pans simmered, all suggestive of some approaching feast.

A white-headed baby lay in the old blue cradle that had rocked seven other babies, now and then lifting his head to look out, like a round, full moon, then subsided to kick and crow contentedly, and suck the rosy apple he had no teeth to bite. Two small boys sat on the wooden settle shelling corn for popping, and picking out the biggest nuts from the goodly store their own hands had gathered in October. Four young girls stood at the long dresser, busily chopping meat, pounding spice, and slicing apples; and the tongues of Tilly, Prue, Roxy, and Rhody went as fast as their hands. Farmer Bassett, and Eph, the oldest boy, were "chorin' 'round" outside, for Thanksgiving was at hand, and all must be in order for that time-honored day.

To and fro, from table to hearth, bustled buxom Mrs. Bassett, flushed and floury, but busy and blithe as the queen bee of this busy little hive should be.

"I do like to begin seasonable and have things to my mind. Thanksgivin' dinners can't be drove, and it does take a sight of victuals to fill all these hungry stomicks," said the good woman, as she gave a vigorous stir to the great kettle of cider apple-sauce, and cast a glance of housewifely pride at the fine array of pies set forth on the buttery shelves.

"Only one more day and then it will be time to eat. I didn't take but one bowl of hasty pudding this morning, so I shall have plenty of room when the nice things come," confided Seth to Sol, as he cracked a large hazel-nut as easily as a squirrel.

"No need of my starvin' beforehand. I *always* have room enough, and I'd like to have Thanksgiving every day," answered Solomon, gloating like a young ogre over the little pig that lay near by, ready for roasting.

*Louisa May Alcott*

"Sakes alive, I don't, boys! It's a marcy it don't come but once a year. I should be worn to a thread-paper with all this extra work atop of my winter-weavin' and spinnin'," laughed their mother as she plunged her plump arms into the long bread-trough and began to knead the dough as if a famine was at hand.

Tilly, the oldest girl, a red-cheeked, black-eyed lass of fourteen, was grinding briskly at the mortar, for spices were costly, and not a grain must be wasted. Prue kept time with the chopper, and the twins sliced away at the apples till their little brown arms ached, for all knew how to work, and did so now with a will.

"I think it's real fun to have Thanksgiving at home. I'm sorry Gran'ma is sick, so we can't go there as usual, but I like to mess 'round here, don't you, girls?" asked Tilly, pausing to take a sniff at the spicy pestle.

"It will be kind of lonesome with only our own folks." "I like to see all the cousins and aunts, and have games, and sing," cried the twins, who were regular little romps, and could run, swim, coast, and shout as well as their brothers.

"I don't care a mite for all that. It will be so nice to eat dinner together, warm and comfortable at home," said quiet Prue, who loved her own cozy nooks like a cat.

"Come, girls, fly 'round and get your chores done, so we can clear away for dinner jest as soon as I clap my bread into the oven," called Mrs. Bassett presently, as she rounded off the last loaf of brown bread which was to feed the hungry mouths that

*Louisa May Alcott*

seldom tasted any other.

"Here's a man comin' up the hill lively!"
"Guess it's Gad Hopkins. Pa told him to bring
a dezzen oranges, if they warn't too high!"
shouted Sol and Seth, running to the door,
while the girls smacked their lips at the
thought of this rare treat, and Baby threw his
apple overboard, as if getting ready for a new
cargo.

But all were doomed to disappointment,
for it was not Gad, with the much-desired
fruit. It was a stranger, who threw himself
off his horse and hurried up to Mr. Bassett in
the yard, with some brief message that made
the farmer drop his ax and look so sober that
his wife guessed at once some bad news had
come; and crying, "Mother's wuss! I know
she is!" out ran the good woman, forgetful

of the flour on her arms and the oven waiting for its most important batch.

The man said old Mr. Chadwick, down to Keene, stopped him as he passed, and told him to tell Mrs. Bassett her mother was failin' fast, and she'd better come today. He knew no more, and having delivered his errand he rode away, saying it looked like snow and he must be jogging, or he wouldn't get home till night.

"We must go right off, Eldad. Hitch up, and I'll be ready in less'n no time," said Mrs. Bassett, wasting not a minute in tears and lamentations, but pulling off her apron as she went in, with her head in a sad jumble of bread, anxiety, turkey, sorrow, haste, and cider apple-sauce.

A few words told the story, and the chil-

dren left their work to help get ready, min-
gling their grief for "Gran'ma" with regrets
for the lost dinner.

"I'm dreadful sorry, dears, but it can't be
helped. I couldn't cook nor eat no way, now,
and if that blessed woman gets better sudden, as she has before, we'll have cause for
thanksgivin', and I'll give you a dinner you
won't forget in a hurry," said Mrs. Bassett, as
she tied on her brown silk pumpkin-hood,
with a sob for the good old mother who had
made it for her.

Not a child complained after that, but ran
about helpfully, bringing moccasins, heat-
ing the footstone, and getting ready for a long
drive, because Gran'ma lived twenty miles
away, and there were no railroads in those
parts to whisk people to and fro like magic.

## An Old Fashioned Thanksgiving

By the time the old yellow sleigh was at the door, the bread was in the oven, and Mrs. Bassett was waiting, with her camlet cloak on, and the baby done up like a small bale of blankets.

"Now, Eph, you must look after the cattle like a man, and keep up the fires, for there's a storm brewin', and neither the children nor dumb critters must suffer," said Mr. Bassett, as he turned up the collar of his rough coat and put on his blue mittens, while the old mare shook her bells as if she preferred a trip to Keene to hauling wood all day.

"Tilly, put extry comfortables on the beds tonight, the wind is so searchin' up chamber. Have the baked beans and Injun-puddin' for dinner, and whatever you do, don't let the boys git at the mince-pies, or you'll have them down sick. I shall come back the minute I can leave Mother. Pa will come tomorrer, anyway, so keep snug and be good. I depend on you, my darter; use your jedgment, and don't let nothin' happen while Mother's away."

"Yes'm, yes'm—good-bye, good-bye!" called the children, as Mrs. Bassett was packed into the sleigh and driven away, leaving a stream of directions behind her.

Eph, the sixteen-year-old boy, immediately put on his biggest boots, assumed a sober, responsible manner, and surveyed his little responsibilities with a paternal air, drolly like his father's. Tilly tied on her mother's bunch of keys, rolled up the sleeves of her homespun gown, and began to order about the younger girls. They soon forgot poor Granny, and found it great fun to keep house all alone, for Mother seldom left home, but ruled her family in the good old-fashioned way. There were no servants, for the little daughters were Mrs. Bassett's only maids, and the stout boys helped their father, all working happily together with no wages but love; learning in the best manner the use of the heads and hands with which they were to make their own way in the world.

The few flakes that caused the farmer to predict bad weather soon increased to a regular snow-storm, with gusts of wind, for up among the hills winter came early and lingered long. But the children were busy, gay, and warm indoors, and never minded the rising gale nor the whirling white storm outside.

Tilly got them a good dinner, and when it was over the two elder girls went to their spinning, for in the kitchen stood the big and little wheels, and baskets of wool-rolls, ready to be twisted into yarn for the winter's knitting, and each day brought its stint of work to the daughters, who hoped to be as thrifty as their mother.

Eph kept up a glorious fire, and superintended the small boys, who popped corn and whittled boats on the hearth; while Roxy and Rhody dressed corn-cob dolls in the settle corner,and Bose, the brindled mastiff, lay on the braided mat, luxuriously warming his old legs. Thus employed, they made a pretty picture, these rosy boys and girls, in their homespun suits, with the rustic toys or tasks which most children nowadays would find very poor or tiresome.

Tilly and Prue sang, as they stepped to and fro, drawing out the smoothly twisted threads to the musical hum of great spinning-wheels. The little girls chattered like magpies over their dolls and the new bed-spread they were planning to make, all white dimity stars on a blue calico ground, as a Christmas present to Ma. The boys roared at Eph's jokes, and had rough and tumble games over Bose, who didn't mind them in the least; and so the afternoon wore pleasantly away.

At sunset the boys went out to feed the cattle, bring in heaps of wood, and lock up for the night, as the lonely farm-house seldom had visitors after dark. The girls got the simple supper of brown bread and milk, baked apples, and a doughnut all 'round as a treat. Then they sat before the fire, the sisters knitting, the brothers with books or games, for Eph loved reading, and Sol and Seth never failed to play a few games of Morris with barley corns, on the little board they had made themselves at one corner of the dresser.

"Read out a piece," said Tilly, from Mother's chair, where she sat in state, finishing off the sixth woolen sock she had knit that month.

"It's the old history book, but here's a bit you might like, since it's about our folks," answered Eph, turning the yellow page to look at a picture of two quaintly dressed children in some ancient castle.

"Yes, read that. I always like to hear about the Lady Matildy I was named for, and Lord Bassett, Pa's great-great-great-grandpa. He's only a farmer now, but it's nice to know we were somebody two or three hundred years ago," said Tilly, bridling and tossing her curly head as she fancied the Lady Matilda might have done.

"Don't read the queer words, 'cause we don't understand 'em. Tell it," commanded Roxy, from the cradle, where she was drowsily cuddled with Rhody.

Well, a long time ago, when Charles the First was in prison, Lord Bassett was a true friend to him," began Eph, plunging into his story without delay. "The Lord had some papers that would have hung a lot of people if the king's enemies got hold of 'em, so when he heard one day, all of a sudden, that soldiers were at the castle-gate to carry him off, he had just time to call his girl to him, and say: 'I may be going to my death, but I won't betray my master. There's no time to burn the papers, and I cannot take them with me; they are hidden in the old leathern chair where I sit. No one knows this but you, and you must guard them till I come or send you a safe messenger to take them away. Promise me to be brave and silent, and I can go without fear.' You see, he wasn't afraid to die, but he *was* to seem a traitor. Lady Matildy promised solemnly, and the words were hardly out of her mouth when the men came in, and her father was carried away a prisoner and sent off to the Tower."

"But she didn't cry; she just called her brother, and sat down in that chair, with her head leaning back on those papers, like a queen, and waited while the soldiers hunted the house over for 'em: wasn't that a smart girl?" cried Tilly, beaming with pride, for she was named for this ancestress, and knew the story by heart.

"I reckon she was scared, though, when the men came swearin' in and asked her if she knew anything about it. The boy did his part then, for he didn't know, and fired up and stood before his sister; and he says, says he, as bold as a lion: 'If my lord had told us where the papers be, we would die before we would betray him. But we are children and know nothing, and it is cowardly of you to try to fright us with oaths and drawn swords!'"

As Eph quoted from the book, Seth planted himself before Tilly, with the long poker in his hand, saying, as he flourished it valiantly:

"Why didn't the boy take his father's sword and lay about him? I would, if any one was ha'sh to Tilly."

"You bantam! He was only a bit of a boy, and couldn't do anything. Sit down and hear the rest of it," commanded Tilly, with a pat on the yellow head, and a private resolve that Seth should have the largest piece of pie at dinner next day, as a reward for his chivalry.

"Well, the men went off after turning the castle out of window, but they said they should come again; so faithful Matildy was full of trouble, and hardly dared to leave the room where the chair stood. All day she sat there, and at night her sleep was so full of fear about it, that she often got up and went to see that all was safe. The servants thought the fright had hurt her wits, and let her be, but Rupert, the boy, stood by her and never was afraid of her queer ways. She was 'a pious maid,' the book says, and often spent the long evenings reading the Bible, with her brother by her, all alone in the great room, with no one to help her bear her secret, and no good news of her father. At last, word came that the king was dead and his friends banished out of England. Then the poor children were in a sad plight, for they had no mother, and the servants all ran away, leaving only one faithful old man to help them."

"But the father did come?" cried Roxy, eagerly.

"You'll see," continued Eph, half telling, half reading.

"Matilda was sure he would, so she sat on

in the big chair, guarding the papers, and no one could get her away, till one day a man came with her father's ring and told her to give up the secret. She knew the ring, but would not tell until she had asked many questions, so as to be very sure, and while the man answered all about her father and the king, she looked at him sharply. Then she stood up and said, in a tremble, for there was something strange about the man: 'Sir, I doubt you in spite of the ring, and I will not answer till you pull off the false beard you wear, that I may see your face and know if you are my father's friend or foe.' Off came the disguise, and Matilda found it was my lord himself, come to take them with him out of England. He was very proud of that faithful girl, I guess, for the old chair still stands in the castle, and the name keeps in the family, Pa says, even over here, where some of the Bassetts came along with the Pilgrims."

"Our Tilly would have been as brave, I know, and she looks like the old picter down to Grandma's, don't she, Eph?" cried Prue, who admired her bold sister very much.

"Well, I think you'd do the settin' part best, Prue, you are so patient. Till would fight like a wild cat, but she can't hold her tongue worth a cent," answered Eph; whereat Tilly pulled his hair, and the story ended with a general frolic.

When the moon-faced clock behind the door struck nine, Tilly tucked up the chil-

dren under the 'extry comfortables,' and
having kissed them all around, as Mother did,
crept into her own nest, never minding the
little drifts of snow that sifted in upon her
coverlet between the shingles of the roof, nor
the storm that raged without.

As if he felt the need of unusual vigilance,
old Bose lay down on the mat before the door,
and pussy had the warm hearth all to herself.
If any late wanderer had looked in at
midnight, he would have seen the fire
blazing up again, and in the
cheerful glow the old cat
blinking her yellow eyes, as
she sat bolt upright beside
the spinning-wheel, like
some sort of household

goblin, guarding the children while they slept.

When they woke, like early birds, it still snowed, but up the little Bassetts jumped, broke the ice in their pitchers, and went down with cheeks glowing like winter appples, after a brisk scramble into their clothes. Eph was off to the barn, and Tilly soon had a great kettle of mush ready, which, with milk warm from the cows, made a wholesome breakfast for the seven hearty children.

"Now about dinner," said the young housekeeper, as the pewter spoons stopped clattering, and the earthen bowls stood empty.

"Ma said, have what we liked, but she didn't expect us to have a real Thanksgiving dinner, because she won't be here to cook it, and we don't know how," began Prue, doubtfully.

"I can roast a turkey and make a pudding as well as anybody, I guess. The pies are all ready, and if we can't boil vegetables and so on, we don't deserve any dinner," cried Tilly, burning to distinguish herself, and bound to enjoy to the utmost her brief authority.

"Yes, yes!" cried all the boys,"let's have a dinner anyway; Ma won't care, and the good victuals will spoil if they ain't eaten right up."

"Pa is coming tonight, so we won't have dinner till late; that will be real genteel and give us plenty of time," added Tilly, suddenly realizing the novelty of the task she had undertaken.

"Did you ever roast a turkey?" asked Roxy,

with an air of deep interest.

"Should you darst to try?" said Rhody, in awe-stricken tone.

"You will see what I can do. Ma said I was to use my jedgment about things, and I'm going to. All you children have got to do is to keep out of the way, and let Prue and me work. Eph, I wish you'd put a fire in the best room, so the little ones can play in there. We shall want the settin' room for the table, and I won't have 'em pickin' 'round when we get things fixed," commanded Tilly, bound to make her short reign a brilliant one.

"I don't know about that. Ma didn't tell us to," began cautious Eph, who felt that his invasion of the sacred parlor was a daring step.

"Don't we always do it Sundays and Thanksgivings? Wouldn't Ma wish the children kept safe and warm anyhow? Can I get up a nice dinner with four rascals under my feet all the time? Come, now, if you want roast turkey and onions, plum-puddin' and mince-pie, you'll have to do as I tell you, and be lively about it."

Tilly spoke with such spirit, and her last suggestion was so irresistible, that Eph gave in, and, laughing good-naturedly, tramped away to heat up the best room, devoutly hoping that nothing serious would happen to punish such audacity.

The young folks delightedly trooped in to destroy the order of that prim apartment with houskeeping under the black horse-hair sofa, "horseback riders" on the arms of the best rocking chair, and an Indian war-dance all over the well-waxed furniture. Eph, finding the society of the peaceful sheep and cows more to his mind than that of two excited sisters, lingered over his chores in the barn as long as possible, and left the girls in peace.

Now Tilly and Prue were in their glory, and as soon as the breakfast things were out of the way, they prepared for a grand cooking-time. They were handy girls, though they had never heard of a cooking school, never touched a piano, and knew nothing of embroidery beyond the samplers which hung framed in the parlor; one ornamented with a pink mourner under a blue weeping- willow, the other with this pleasing verse, each word being done in a different color, which gave the effect of a distracted rainbow:

"This sampler neat was worked by me,
In my twelfth year, Prudence B."

Both rolled up their sleeves, put on their largest aprons, and got out all the spoons, dishes, pots, and pans they could find, "so as to have everything handy," as Prue said.

"Now, sister, we'll have dinner at five; Pa will be here by that time if he is coming to-night, and be so surprised to find us all ready, for he won't have had very nice victuals if Gran'ma is so sick," said Tilly importantly. "I shall give the children a piece at noon" (Tilly meant luncheon); doughnuts and cheese, with apple-pie and cider will please 'em. There's beans for Eph; he likes cold pork, so we won't stop to warm it up, for there's lots to do, and I don't mind saying to you I'm dreadful dubersome about the turkey."

"It's all ready but the stuffing, and roasting is as easy as can be. I can baste first rate. Ma always likes to have me, I'm so patient and stiddy, she says," answered Prue, for the responsibility of this great undertaking did not rest upon her, so she took a cheerful view of things.

"I know but it's the stuffin' that troubles me," said Tilly, rubbing her round elbows as she eyed the immense fowl laid out on a platter before her. "I don't know how much I want, nor what sort of yarbs to put in, and he's so awful big, I'm kind of afraid of him."

"I ain't! I fed him all summer, and he never gobbled at me. I feel real mean to be thinking of gobbling him, poor old chap," laughed Prue, patting her departed pet with an air of mingled affection and appetite.

"Well I'll get the puddin' off my mind fust, for it ought to bile all day. Put the big kettle on, and see that the spit is clean, while I get ready."

Prue obediently tugged away at the crane, with its black hooks, from which hung the iron tea-kettle and three-legged pot; then she settled the long spit in the grooves made for it in the tall andirons, and put the dripping-pan underneath, for in those days meat was roasted as it should be, not baked in ovens.

Meantime Tilly attacked the plum-pudding.

She felt pretty sure of coming out right, here, for she had seen her mother do it so many times, it looked very easy. So in went suet and fruit; all sorts of spice, to be sure she got the right ones, and brandy instead of wine. But she forgot both sugar and salt, and tied it in the cloth so tightly that it had no room to swell, so it would come out as heavy as lead and as hard as a cannon-ball, if the bag did not burst and spoil it all. Happily unconscious of these mistakes, Tilly popped it into the pot, and proudly watched it bobbing about before she put the cover on and left it to its fate.

"I can't remember what flavorin' Ma puts in," she said, when she had got her bread well soaked for the stuffing. "Sage and onions and apple-sauce go with goose, but I can't feel sure of anything but pepper and salt for a turkey."

"Ma puts in some kind of mint, I know, but I forget whether it is spearmint, peppermint, or pennyroyal," answered Prue, in a tone of doubt, but trying to show her knowledge of "yarbs," or, at least, of their names.

"Seems to me it's sweet marjoram or summer savory. I guess we'll put both in, and then we are sure to be right. The best is up garret; you run and get some, while I mash the bread," commanded Tilly, diving into the mess.

Away trotted Prue, but in her haste she got catnip and wormwood, for the garret was darkish, and Prue's little nose was so full of the smell of the onions she had been peeling, that everything smelt of them. Eager to be of use, she pounded up the herbs and scattered the mixture with a liberal hand into the bowl.

"It doesn't smell jest right, but I suppose it will when it is cooked," said Tilly, as she filled the empty stomach, that seemed aching for food, and sewed it up with the blue yarn, which happened to be handy. She forgot to tie down his legs and wings, but she set him by till his hour came, well satisfied with her work.

"Shall we roast the little pig, too? I think he'd look nice with a necklace of sausages, as Ma fixed one last Christmas," asked Prue, elated with their success.

"I couldn't do it. I loved that little pig, and

cried when he was killed. I should feel as if I was roasting the baby," answered Tilly, glancing toward the buttery where piggy hung, looking so pink and pretty it certainly did seem cruel to eat him.

It took a long time to get all the vegetables ready, for, as the cellar was full, the girls thought they would have every sort. Eph helped, and by noon all was ready for cooking, and the cranberry-sauce, a good deal scorched, was cooling in the lean-to.

Luncheon was a lively meal, and doughnuts and cheese vanished in such quantities that Tilly feared no one would have an appetite for her sumptuous dinner. The boys assured her they would be starving by five o'clock, and Sol mourned bitterly over the little pig that was not to be served up.

"Now you all go and coast, while Prue and I set the table and get out the best chiny," said Tilly, bent on having her dinner look well, no matter what its other failings might be.

Out came the rough sleds, on went the round hoods, old hats, red cloaks, and moc- casins, and away trudged the four younger Bassetts, to disport themselves in the snow, and try the ice down by the old mill, where the great wheel turned and splashed so mer- rily in the summer-time.

Eph took his fiddle and scraped away to his heart's content in the parlor, while the girls, after a short rest, set the table and made all ready to dish up the dinner when that exciting moment came. It was not at all the sort of table we see now, but would look very plain and countrified to us, with its green-handled knives and two-pronged steel forks; its red and white china, and pewter platters, scoured till they shone, with mugs and spoons to match, and a brown mug for the cider. The cloth was coarse, but white as snow, and the little maids had seen the blue-eyed flax grow, out of which their mother wove the linen they had watched and watered while it bleached in the green meadow. They had no napkins and little silver; but the best tankard and Ma's few wedding spoons were set forth in state. Nuts and apples at the corners gave an air, and the place of honor was left in the middle for the oranges yet to come.

"Don't it look beautiful?" said Prue, when they paused to admire the general effect.

"Pretty nice, I think. I wish Ma could see how well we can do it," began Tilly, when a loud howling startled both girls, and sent them flying to the window. The short afternoon had passed so quickly that twilight had come before they knew it, and now, as they looked out through the gathering dusk, they saw four small figures tearing up the road, to come bursting in, all screaming at once:"The bear, the bear! Eph, get the gun! He's coming, he's coming!"

Eph had dropped his fiddle, and got down his gun before the girls could calm the children enough to tell their story, which they did in a somewhat incoherent manner.

"Down in the holler, coastin', we heard a growl," began Sol, with his eyes as big as saucers. "I see him fust lookin' over the wall," roared Seth, eager to get his share of honor.

"Awful big and shaggy," quavered Roxy, clinging to Tilly while Rhody hid in Prue's skirts, and piped out: "His great paws kept clawing at us, and I was so scared my legs would hardly go."

"We ran away as fast as we could go, and he come growling after us. He's awful hungry, and he'll eat every one of us if he gets in," continued Sol, looking about him for a safe retreat.

"Oh, Eph, don't let him eat us," cried both little girls, flying upstairs to hide under their mother's bed, as their surest shelter.

"No danger of that, you little geese. I'll shoot him as soon as he comes. Get out of the way, boys," and Eph raised the window to get good aim.

"There he is! Fire away, and don't miss!" cried Seth, hastily following Sol, who had climbed to the top of the dresser as a good perch from which to view the approaching fray.

Prue retired to the hearth as if bent on dying at her post rather than desert the turkey, now "browning beautiful," as she expressed it. But Tilly boldly stood at the open window, ready to lend a hand if the enemy proved too much for Eph.

All had seen bears, but none had ever come so near before, and even brave Eph felt that the big brown beast slowly trotting up the door-yard was an unusually formidable specimen. He was growling horribly, and stopped now and then as if to rest and shake himself.

"Get the ax, Tilly, and if I should miss, stand ready to keep him off while I load again," said Eph, anxious to kill his first bear in style and alone; a girl's help didn't count.

Tilly flew for the ax, and was at her brother's side by the time the bear was near enough to be dangerous. He stood on his hind legs, and seemed to sniff with relish the savory odors that poured out of the window.

"Fire, Eph!" cried Tilly, firmly.

"Wait till he rears again. I'll get a better shot, then," answered the boy, while Prue covered her ears to shut out the bang, and the small boys cheered from their dusty refuge up among the pumpkins.

But a very singular thing happened next, and all who saw it stood amazed, for suddenly Tilly threw down the ax, flung open the door, and ran straight into the arms of the bear, who stood erect to receive her, while his growlings changed to a loud "Haw,haw!" that startled the children more than the retort of a gun.

"It's Gad Hopkins, tryin' to fool us!" cried Eph, much disgusted at the loss of his prey, for these hardy boys loved to hunt, and prided themselves on the number of wild animals and birds they could shoot in a year.

"Oh, Gad, how could you scare us so?" laughed Tilly, still held fast in one shaggy arm of the bear, while the other drew a dozen oranges from some deep pocket in the buffalo-skin coat, and fired them into the kitchen with such a good aim that Eph ducked, Prue screamed, and Sol and Seth came down much quicker than they went up.

"Wal, you see I got upsot over yonder, and the old horse went home while I was floundering in a drift, so I tied on the buffalers to tote'em easy, and come along till I see the children playin' in the holler. I jest meant to give 'em a little scare, but they run like partridges, and I kep' up the joke to see how Eph would like this sort of company," and Gad haw-hawed again.

"You'd have had a warm welcome if we hadn't found you out. I'd have put a bullet through you in a jiffy, old chap," said Eph, coming out to shake hands with the young giant, who was only a year or two older than himself.

"Come in and set up to dinner with us. Prue and I have done it all ourselves, and Pa will be along soon, I reckon," cried Tilly, trying to escape.

"Couldn't, no ways. My folks will think I'm dead ef I don't get along home, sence the horse and sleigh have gone ahead empty. I've done my arrant and had my joke; now I want my pay, Tilly," and Gad took a hearty kiss from the rosy cheeks of his "little sweetheart," as he called her. His own cheeks tingled with the smart slap she gave him as she ran away, calling out that she hated bears and would bring her ax next time.

"I ain't afeared; your sharp eyes found me out; and ef you run into a bear's arms you must expect a hug," answered Gad, as he pushed back the robe and settled his fur cap more becomingly.

"I should have known you in a minute if I hadn't been asleep when the girls squalled. You did it well, though, and I advise you not to try it again in a hurry, or you'll get shot," said Eph, as they parted, he rather crestfallen and Gad in high glee.

"My sakes alive—the turkey is burnt on one side, and the kettles have biled over so the pies I put to warm are all ashes!" scolded Tilly, as the flurry subsided and she remembered her dinner.

"Well, I can't help it. I couldn't think of victuals when I expected to be eaten alive myself, could I?" pleaded poor Prue, who had tumbled into the cradle when the rain of oranges began.

Tilly laughed, and all the rest joined in, so good humor was restored, and the spirits of the younger ones were revived by sucks from the one orange which passed from hand to hand with great rapidity while the older girls dished up the dinner. They were just struggling to get the pudding out of the cloth when

Roxy called out,

"Here's Pa!"

"There's folks with him," added Rhody.

"Lots of "em! I see two big sleighs chock full," shouted Seth, peering through the dusk.

"It looks like a semintary. Guess Gramma's dead and come up to be buried here," said Sol, in a solemn tone. This startling suggestion made Tilly, Prue, and Eph hasten to look out, full of dismay at such an ending of their festival.

"If that is a funeral, the mourners are uncommon jolly," said Eph, drily, as merry voices and loud laughter broke the white silence without.

"I see Aunt Cinthy, and Cousin Hetty— and there's Mose and Amos. I do declare,

Pa's bringin' 'em all home to have some fun here," cried Prue, as she recognized one familiar face after another.

"Oh, my patience! Ain't I glad I got dinner, and don't I hope it will turn out good!" exclaimed Tilly, while the twins pranced with delight, and the small boys roared:

"Hooray for Pa! Hooray for Thanksgivin'!"

The cheer was answered heartily, and in came Father, Mother, Baby, aunts and cousins, all in great spirits, and all much surprised to find such a festive welcome awaiting them.

"Ain't Gran'ma dead at all?" asked Sol, in the midst of the kissing and hand-shaking.

"Bless your heart, no! It was all a mistake of old Mr. Chadwick's. He's as deaf as an adder, and when Mrs. Brooks told him

Mother was mendin' fast, and she wanted me to come down today, certain sure, he got the message all wrong, and give it to the fust person passin' in such a way as to scare me' most to death, and send us down in a hurry. Mother was sittin' up as chirk as you please, and dreadful sorry you didn't all come."

"So to keep the house quiet for her, and give you a taste of the fun, your Pa fetched us all up to spend the evenin', and we are goin' to have a jolly time on't, to jedge by the looks of things," said Aunt Cinthy, briskly finishing the tale when Mrs. Bassett paused for want of breath.

"What in the world put it into your head we was comin', and set you to gettin' up such a supper?" asked Mr. Bassett, looking about him, well pleased and much surprised at the plentiful table.

Tilly modestly began to tell, but the others broke in and sang her praises in a sort of chorus, in which bears, pigs, pies, and oranges were oddly mixed. Great satisfaction was expressed by all, and Tilly and Prue were so elated by the commendation of Ma and the aunts, that they set forth their dinner, sure everything was perfect.

But when eating began, which it did the moment wraps were off, then their pride got a fall; for the first person who tasted the stuffing (it was big cousin Mose, and that made it harder to bear) nearly choked over the bitter morsel.

"Tilly Bassett, whatever made you put

wormwood and catnip in your stuffin'?" demanded Ma, trying not to be too severe, for all the rest were laughing, and Tilly looked ready to cry.

"I did it," said Prue, nobly taking all the blame, which caused Pa to kiss her on the spot, and declare that it didn't do a mite of harm, for the turkey was all right.

"I never see onions cooked better. All the vegetables is well done, and the dinner a credit to you, my dears," declared Aunt Cinthy, with her mouth full of the fragrant vegetables she praised.

The pudding was an utter failure, inspite of the blazing brandy in which it lay—as hard as one of the stone balls on Squire Dunkin's great gate. It was speedily whisked out of sight, and all fell upon the pies, which were perfect. But Tilly and Prue were much depressed, and didn't recover their spirits till the dinner was over and the evening fun well under way.

"Blind-man's buff," "Hunt the slipper," "Come, Philander," and other lively games soon set every one bubbling over with jollity, and when Eph struck up "Money Musk" on his fiddle, old and young fell into their places for a dance. All down the long kitchen they stood, Mr. and Mrs. Bassett at the top, the twins at the bottom, and then away they went, heeling and toeing, cutting pigeon-wings, and taking their steps in a way that would convulse modern children with their new-fangled romps called dancing. Mose and

Tilly covered themselves with glory by the vigor with which they kept it up, till fat Aunt Cinthy fell into a chair, breathlessly declaring that a very little of such excercise was enough for a woman of her "heft."

Apples and cider, chat and singing, finished the evening, and after a grand kissing all round, the guests drove away in the clear moonlight which came just in time to cheer their long drive.

When the jingle of the last bell had died away, Mr. Bassett said soberly, as they stood together on the hearth: "Children, we have special cause to be thankful that the sorrow we expected was changed into joy, so we'll read a chapter 'fore we go to bed, and give thanks where thanks is due."

Then Tilly set out the light-stand with the big Bible on it, and a candle on each side, and all sat quietly in the fire-light, smiling as they listened with happy hearts to the sweet old words that fit all times and seasons so beautifully.

When the good-nights were over, and the children in bed, Prue put her arm around Tilly and whispered tenderly, for she felt her shake, and was sure she was crying:

"Don't mind about the old stuffin' and puddin', deary—nobody cared, and Ma said we really did do surprisin' well for such young girls."

The laughter Tilly was trying to smother broke out then, and was so infectious, Prue could not help joining her, even before she knew the cause of the merriment.

"I was mad about the mistakes, but don't care enough to cry. I'm laughing to think how Gad fooled Eph and I found him out. I thought Mose and Amos would have died over it when I told them, it was so funny," explained Tilly, when she got her breath.

"I was so scared that when the first orange hit me, I thought it was a bullet, and scrabbled into the cradle as fast as I could. It was real mean to frighten the little ones so," laughed Prue, as Tilly gave a growl.

Here a smart rap on the wall of the next room caused a sudded lull in the fun, and Mrs. Bassett's voice was heard, saying warningly, "Girls, go to sleep immediate, or you'll wake the baby."

## *An Old Fashioned Thanksgiving*

"Yes'm," answered two meek voices, and after a few irrepressible giggles, silence reigned, broken only by an occasional snore from the boys, or the soft scurry of mice in the buttery, taking their part in this old-fashioned Thanksgiving.

# APPLEWOOD BOOKS
*BRINGING THE PAST ALIVE*

*TIMELESS ADVICE & ENTERTAINMENT*
*FROM AMERICANS WHO CAME BEFORE US*

❧

*George Washington on Manners*
*Benjamin Franklin on Money*
*Lydia Maria Child on Raising Children*
*Henry David Thoreau on Walking*

*&*

*Many More Distinctive Classics*
*Now Available Again*

❧

*At finer bookstores*
*& gift shops or from:*

APPLEWOOD BOOKS
Box 365
Bedford, MA 01730

CPSIA information can be obtained
at www.ICGtesting.com
Printed in the USA
BVOW04s2005211116
468421BV00034B/2/P